Anatomy of a Whale

Matt Barnard

The Onslaught Press

Published in Oxford by The Onslaught Press
11 Ridley Road, OX4 2QJ
20 March 2018

ISBN: **978-1-912111-58-9**

The title on the front cover is set in **MARUJO** by Ricardo Marcin & Erica Jung,
the author's name & back cover texts in Akira Kobayashi's **DIN Next**,
poems and titles in Jean François Porchez's Le Monde Livre,
with title page & end matter in his **Le Monde Sans**,

Printed & bound by Lightning Source

To my family

9 A Lamp Shop
10 Please Follow the Yellow Line
11 Eel
12 The Day Twilight Went on for Days
13 Border Patrol
14 Vision of Heaven
15 Wedding at Elgin
16 What the Water Gave Kahlo
17 The Scribes Bewail the Earth's Circumference
18 Southampton in Paris
19 The Baker's Tale
20 Cows Under a Dark Sky
22 The Counterfeit Jew
23 The Old Whaler, Jonah
24 Hairy Panic
25 The Art of Making Weight
26 Dogdom
27 St Francis and the Animals
28 Portrait of a Dead Girl
30 An Experiment on a Bird in the Air Pump
31 Company
32 Two Beotian Women
33 Narcisse
34 Washing Day
35 Intellectual Property
36 Our Neighbour's Cows

37 Crows
38 Gifts of the Magi
39 The Census of Quirinius
40 Robin's Last Arrow
41 Learning Magic
42 A Portrait of the Artist as a Sasquatch
44 The Sore Thumb
45 The Gift
46 Noah to God
47 The Anaesthetist
48 My Son's Heritage
50 Bride and Groom Consume One Another
51 Dance Mosquito
   Carcasses
52   *Fallen Angels*
53   *Issigonis's Dream*
54   *Anatomy of a Whale*
55 River in Spate
56 The Poet's Voice
57 Skating at Earith
58 You're Letting Your Hair Go Grey Again
59 The Bends
60 A Gibbous Moon

63 Acknowledgements

A Lamp Shop

Alone on the high street, the window of the lamp shop
still blazes, still announces itself to the world:
I am a Lamp Shop, here are my goods for sale.
The street is empty, a cold wind with the sting
of hail or sleet in it bullies its way along the pavement,
past the other shops brooding behind their iron grills.
The betting shop is unwilling to accept a late night wager,
the 7-Eleven has put away its sherbet and Special Brew.
There's just me to witness the show from the car window,
only me to wonder why all the bulbs are lit through the night
with no soul in view, only the town drunk hunkering down
in the doorwell opposite, his back turned to the light.

Please Follow the Yellow Line

The old are here, cluttering up corridors
that have no windows and that lead to rooms
which also have no windows. The old and infirm.

We are a motley crowd, we have missing teeth
and excess weight. Some of us hear
through fathoms of water. Sometimes we fail

to understand what is expected of us
and we think it matters. It feels like it matters.
There is a code that is spoken slowly.

The woman at reception tries to explain
and we all listen in expectantly, just in case.
I think you need Lung Function. Lung Function.

Eel

Dark river of itself, curled in the bottom of the creel,
the small myth was an absence, a light taker,
pulsing with malevolence, its oily body slick
with power and potential, head, tail, middle
a single unremitting story told to the end.

None would put his hand in, tempt the malicious eye
or risk springing the trap of its jaws. Even its name,
the mysterious double e, defied us, bled sound.
Neither fish nor animal, we knew elvers would cross
fields and roads to reach the sea. Could he be a god?

Three days they forgot about him in the bucket.
He baked in the sun, skin drying brown,
contemplating the distant blue of the sky,
until one took pity and brought him down to the sea,
uncurled his body and with tender fingers

sluiced the water through his gills.
How it must have felt, the prisoner released
into the light, Houdini cheating the burning rope —
the thin triumphant smile, the vengeful gleam,
before he disappeared into the blackness of himself.

The Day Twilight Went on for Days

That day the balance held, like the skin of water
on a jar or glass filled to the very top, above the top,

the sun poised just below horizon, the golden hour
stretched out like a cat. Civil twilight wasn't followed

by nautical twilight or astronomical twilight, the sky
didn't lose that darkening blue that is still blue,

not blue-black, or nearly black. The stars, ready
in the wings, limbering up like luminous ballerinas,

had to wait to enter from stage right, and the moon
was a woman, unhurried, holding her face in her hand.

Border Patrol

First they made me empty my heart. My parents laid out side by side. Papa still in his stupid hat, mama in the dress she wore at the last wedding we all went to.

Next they made me empty my conscience. One brother, younger, left behind. I knew they'd be coming and I didn't go back to warn him. I hid in the shadows, and took my chance to escape when they'd gone.

And then they made me empty my memories. Anna at the architect's party where she got so drunk we had to stop the taxi on the way home so she could throw up by the side of the road.

Lastly they asked me to empty my faith. A house with a small garden where you can sit in the evenings and listen to the trains. Neighbours you aren't afraid of.

Finally they said I was free to go. I thought of leaving it all behind, but I'm like a man whose suit is stretched out of shape by all the things he keeps in his pockets.

He complains, but he cannot bear to buy a new one.

Vision of Heaven

Is it this humdrum vision of heaven
seen through the cartoon-eye of the plane
   its drooping eyelid opened
    that makes us so afraid
  to fly? A landscape known to painters
who worked for weeks, years on their backs
   to make chapel ceilings resound
  with glory. What would they say
   to see their inspiration laid so bare
  seen even by those who, like us, fly
   cattle-class, edified only
by flight attendants who mark the experience
   with worn-out rituals before
  the vessel turns to face the runway
which records each black tyre-mark of
  every coming and going, who barely
    bother to strap themselves in
  before the sudden, unearthly acceleration
that stretches time's seams near to breaking
   and makes us airborne? Up here
the air hums, the trolley chinks its way
along the aisle selling synthetic perfume
   and expensive watches while
  like children, foreheads pressed against
the inch-thick panes, afraid someone might catch us
   at it, shyly we stare and stare.

Wedding at Elgin

i.m. HT

December has ravaged the sky, time
broken the cathedral. We shiver

among its freestanding walls.
Someone has brought whiskey

in a brushed-chrome hip flask.
The good liquid burns our throats

as the bride and groom follow
a line of cracked flagstones

down what was once the central aisle.
The mother of the bride is on hand

for last minute adjustments, fingers
going numb. How was she, any

of us, to know it was a sign?
That when the couple rode off

on horseback into the mist
and guests fled back down south

she would be left alone in this ruin
stumbling through its empty spaces

trying to reconstruct arches
and towers from shadows in the air?

What the Water Gave Kahlo

As she sinks down into the water her breasts
float free as jellyfish, her pubic hair lifts
and her swollen foot burns like hot coals.

Diego's there, her laughing monkey, shaving
in his socks and suspenders, his cut-throat razor
sending shards of light around the room, his penis

curled inside its shell like a hermit crab.
She imagines she's a giant submerged in a lake
in the mountains of the Sierra Madre. She imagines

she's the most famous artist in the world.
She remembers Benito, what it was like
to have the dictator whisper murderous nothings

in her ear, while the wind made the sails
of his boat stretch taut against its sheets.
She wonders what it's like to have a rope

around your neck. Do you come before you die?
The blue house leans against a blue sky, waiting.
She holds her breath until the visions appear.

The room fills up with stream. Diego can't shave
any more, so sits on the edge of the bath
and dips his hand into the water, into her world.

The Scribes Bewail the Earth's Circumference

O, our maps, our beautiful maps!
Curse him, Galileo, curse the old, wretched, heartless fool!

May his land burn in summer fires.
May his children suckle from sows' teats.
May his people turn from him, ignore his cries in the desert,
marry into other tribes, recognise other fathers,
and worship at heathen shrines.
May his wives satisfy so many men as there are fish in the sea.

O, why did he do it?
Why spoil these pages leafed with gold?

Are we no more to him than beggars at his door,
dogs feasting on scraps from his table?

We, who buried our heads.
We, who wrought vellum sacred.
We, who defended the faith, his faith.
We, who laboured under vaulted ceilings.

Southampton in Paris

The Queen commands me back in London, but I
have four Queens here that demand my attention,
four Queens to pair with four Kings, if only
luck would play his part. This table's battlefield
is all I need, and drink and willing girls.

Why think about tomorrow, with its chances fickle
as the dice and cards? Screw it all, screw friends,
screw wives in Fleet, screw the Dowager Countess
and her late-flowering lust, screw the court's pet,
that gentleman always ready with a sly word.

To all those who need me, I say find another.
To all those who want me, love another.
What do I owe to any man or to any state,
what do I care if I lose my hand or head?
Let all that rotten country go to hell—

O, I know, the 'wright, the 'wright, the 'wright!

The Baker's Tale

Heat, dry heat, heat like a wall his belly's
pressed against as he works and sweats. The rest
of London sleeps. He works alone, now loading
bread into ovens, now kneading the next batch.
Outside, he hears plague with its horse's head
and rats with beady politician's eyes
scratch at the door. This city stinks, he mumbles,
wiping a hand across a reddening forehead,
best tear it down and start again, or better
still turn them all to stone, or salt, every
frog, gypsy, wop the King lets in — how'd
he think the plague got in? He shoots a look
across the bench, but no-one's there, there's too
few honest working men like him, he thinks,
too few, so sets his hands to dough again.
The sun tilts over the horizon, as
the morning bustle starts and life that's locked
away at night stretches in the sun.
Baker stands at the door scowling, the smell
of freshly baked bread lifts into the street.
Some days he sees the whole of London burning.

Cows Under a Dark Sky

I go to see the cows
in the bottom field,
to observe
their solemn faces
before the rain falls,

but they themselves
are a dark sky,
a storm
waiting to happen
when the herd decides to move

or when startled,
the sudden bulk of them skipping,
though an animal
less built for skipping would be
hard to imagine.

And have you seen the rain
they make?
A single brass
stair rod scalding the air—
that's how the gods
should piss!

But step between
the wires and
they become a landscape,
boulders
dropped by giant hands.

I stand in their realm
alive to the air's
unspent charge,
entranced
by the violet in their flaring nostrils
& the widening sky.

The Counterfeit Jew

In answer to the Jewish question I answer 'no'
though by my brow, my eyes, my nose you'd be forgiven
     for thinking so;

for even in a room of Jews on Sabbath Friday, one asked
if I was one, and said of all the men there, I was the one
     you wouldn't ask.

I followed their rituals, took water like proper Jews
do, like my father's mother's father must have done, but
     I watch the news

and see stone-throwers nightly face the tanks, and lies
and wonder who my lost people are who can only
     see one side, eye

for an eye, ten deaths for a death. Who is counterfeit,
those who lose their lands, their histories, or the lessons
     they beget?

The Old Whaler, Jonah

Was it vindictiveness? Did the old prophet's past
come back to haunt him, making him take to lug
and spear and venture out again to those waters?
Or did he find an old friend beached, the bulk
that kept him safe so long, now as deadly as any harpoon,
and watch as he was stripped down till all that was left
were bones like words without the freight of meaning?
No one knew, but sure enough when I went down
to the white house stubbornly facing the sea, where all
the others turn their backs against the gales, there
propped against the door was a tusk of bone twice
a man's height, moss creeping up its whale-grey length.
And through the windows I counted six vertebrae
littering his room. I was afraid. But come
to ask him for his blessing I could hardly turn back
and leave my guests to watch their food go cold,
so I knocked and waited. And still waited,
but eventually he came, the famous mass of hair
crowned now by a fist of pale skin above a squint.
Of course, I wanted to ask about the bones,
and whether it was true he'd taken each block of flesh
and roasted it over an open fire. But I was afraid,
so I stuck to my task, and asked him for my favour.
When he spoke I did hear thunder, and when he raised
his arms, the sea gathered itself once more, the wind howled
and I could see the old man hadn't lost his touch.

He waved me off with bony hands worn smooth
from truth-telling, a smile back on his face.
What does a retired prophet do? Go mad, with dreams
that no one needs but he cannot stop? I turned and ran.

Hairy Panic

When hairy panic rolled into Wagga Wagga
and filled up doorways and smothered cars
and overwhelmed the gardens, it felt like
the world had ended and not ended too.
It felt like the whole town was under water.

People didn't know what to do with themselves,
whether to fold up their lives and leave them
in the back of a drawer. To shed their loose skin
and run naked up the high street, into the banks,
up and down the whole-food aisles in supermarkets.

Even the animals were lost, dogs gone wild,
yellow big heads mooning about the place.
One man tried to shoot himself, but used
the wrong end of a banana. Someone announced
the second coming, but no one believed them.

As lazy-eyed Pete said, a case of too many
kangaroos loose in the top paddock, mate.

The Art of Making Weight

It was the day the snow fell
                    in individual flakes and macaques
              howled at a daytime moon
and the wolves hung
                  like Hoover
        bags in the crook
                        of an ageing oak tree
the day of the elephant, dark-grey
                    moving against the light-grey
of the concrete wall
                the upturned saucers of her feet
swift and silent among the sawdust
                    the hands
                        of a man playing chase-
the-lady, a rain stick turned
                  before it finishes
and more than anything
                    I wanted to learn her
          secret, the art of making weight seem
weightlessness.

Dogdom

Dogs in their dogdom
are free from human laws and doggy laws

running in mad circles on the sand,
driven berserk by sea-wind howling in their conch ears,

their over-sized, mongrel-rabbit ears.
One, in retirement, one-eyed, is an abandoned sheepskin coat

steaming and dragging itself under an up-turned skiff
behind a beach café. Others zigzag

between people on the promenade,
getting under the feet of the runner sweating through his vest,

then making love with their pink wet worms,
one astride another like pigs.

They're absent minded as drunks
until in a frenzy of teeth they're on a small white dog,

balled round it, slaver making their voices husky
as they grab for any piece of flesh,

jerking its body around like a kite
that's torn at by the wind, and I want to grow big flappy ears,

have my jaw lengthen and my mouth
fill with teeth, abandon myself to their savage blood let,

then run on the beach with my tail up
and my tongue covered in fur.

St Francis and the Animals

After de Zurbarán

Lord, he prays, give these hands strength
To do your work, to punish the sinner,
To bring your vengeance to those who deserve it,
To the enemies of your church, your mission.
Let me not rest until I have hunted down all
That would defy your will, let me not shudder
And turn away from my duty lest my hands
Become soiled with the blood of the damned.
Rather would I have you strike me down here
And leave no remnant of my soul upon the earth.

And the birds and the beasts, the wolf and the bear,
The vulture and the raptor, come unto him,
For they know him for one of their own.

Portrait of a Dead Girl

After all this time it felt good
to put on my old body, to slip
my elbows into their corners,
feel the stocky shape of my legs,
the dark crown of my frizzy hair,
to have my face settle on my face.

Now I hang over their bed and face
the window, its curtains good
and thick, the velvet matted as hair
but with holes enough to let light slip
through in shafts, as if they were legs
of another girl hiding in the corner.

I watch them in all the corners
of the house, my mother whose face
reminds her of me (unlike her legs
which were always slim) my good
sister who keeps busy, but slips
out when she can, tying back her hair —

I was always jealous of her hair —
so she can swim between corners
of rock, like a molecule slipping
in and out of test tubes, her face
raw from the cold. It does her good
she says, but one time her legs

turned to marble, like the legs
of some dead statue and her hair
felt like a sheet of ice. What good
can come of it? My mother cornered
her when she came back, her own face
almost as white, what if you slip

and fall, because it's easy to slip
on wet rock, easy for your legs
to go from under you. My sister's face
was framed then by her wet hair
but she couldn't look into the corners
of her heart and see it was no good.

It's no good, I know, when you slip
into corners, hiding away your face
unable to feel your legs, touch your hair.

An Experiment on a Bird in the Air Pump

Would you tell us if you could,
Mr Wright of Derby, whether
the cockatoo, one useless wing
outstretched, died like Boyle's

with her Breast upward, her Head
downwards, and her Neck awry?
Would you reveal the identity
of the lovers lost in each others'

eyes, the words the father chose
to explain away his daughters'
fears, the thoughts of the pair
of stoics from the Lunar circle?

And what would you tell, Joseph,
of that natural philosopher,
showman in his dressing gown,
grey hair maned around his head,

his hooded eyes inscrutable,
of his boy who wonders whether
it's worth the effort of lowering
the gilded cage a second time?

Company

Pity Midas, fair enough, but pity too his
lesser-known brother, everything he touched

turned not to gold, milking the sun's rays
like a goatherd, but to dust, to shit, to stuff

that would make you turn your face away,
hook one hand over your nose and crouch down

to retch. His was an unasked-for blessing,
a curse brought about not by arrogance or stupidity

but sheer ill luck. At his approach the villagers,
zebra-striped under the sway of an old palm tree,

would snatch up their brown-eyed babes
and run for the woods, leaving their earthenware

to crack in fires. Even the birds and beasts
would recognise his scent and show a hoof

or a brightly-coloured wing. Truly he walked alone,
not even the other's misery for company.

Two Beotian Women

Freedom is dancing without a care in the world.
They think us foolish, that we let the wind
blow our senses away, that we have wind-madness,
that our heads are full of wind which is full of nothing.
They are afraid of the wild hair we grow under
our arms and between our legs, of the thrill
we get from the loose silks that press against
our generous chests, that fly out letting the world
see our milky thighs and misshapen toes. Let them
disapprove, let them make a curse of our name,
let them hold us up to ridicule among the people
of Hellas. We don't hear them, we don't care,
we're lost in the ecstasy of our own kingdom,
lost to the unparalleled pleasures of the flesh.

Narcisse

This is what divinity looks like. Demi-divinity
if you must. But to you it's the same thing,
almost the same, anyhow. Do you like my tail?
It is immensely long and I am immensely proud
of it, but who wouldn't be? It is almost my favourite
part of my splendid anatomy. My ears, are they not fine too?
The way they rise to points and complement my long
green hair. Yes, you are correct, they do echo my sharp fingers,
the nails trimmed to points. And I promise you,
you won't be disappointed when you see my appendage,
nor, my dear, when you discover what I can do with it!

Washing Day

Oriental vowels cut the air, making my
　　　ears bleed, and the washing machine still rocks;
inside the regular thumping of a desperate man
trying to get out. The top is
　　　undulating, like it might be
resting on

water. The hot air stuffs the room. Dryers stare
　　　with absent eyes. The elegant Chinese
woman — beret, cream jumper (the cuffs slightly over hands),
yellow scarf, black skirt — is holding
　　　the stringy washing with fingers
like chopsticks.

Dances on nimble feet, lip curled, but only
　　　slightly, tiptoes briskly from one machine
to another, swapping, emptying, filling. The silent fall
of her feet doesn't interrupt
　　　the circular noise. The tumbling
underwear,

tea towels, dresses, shirts are continuously
　　　falling. The curve of the hip mirrors the
hidden weight of breasts, and the air is full of the static
prickle of things unsaid. She leaves.
　　　The machines stop their tumbling, and
all is still.

Intellectual Property

Who owns the thought of this house in my head?
Where are its deeds? Where are the boundaries?
Locked up in a cabinet in an imaginary office?

What about my desires radiating like hot-plates,
and emotions going off like party-poppers?
Who owns the thought of this house in my head,

who has the right to flick the switches, make it burn
in the darkness? And the ideas that I keep
locked up in a cabinet in an imaginary office,

do I have the only key? Are they mine alone or shared
with someone else, the landlord of my mind perhaps
who owns the thought of this house in my head?

Once I thought of what someone else was thinking,
was that theft, trespass, what if they catch me, will I be
locked up in a cabinet in an imaginary office?

And better not mention sex. That woman's hip,
another's breasts, those must be worth a pretty penny
to whoever owns the thought of this house in my head,
locked up in a cabinet in an imaginary office.

Our Neighbour's Cows

Our neighbour brings her cows home
in six-o'clock light. She calls their names:
Jane after Fonda, Bette after Davis,
Joan after Fontaine (not Crawford),
Marilyn, there is only one Marilyn.

They sway after her, sashay up the hill
and conga along the lane. At home
the new tin roof on her blackhouse winks
back at the sun while slowly raising
its cloak of stars like a diorama.

Sometimes I see her walk down to where
the fishing boats are tethered to the shore,
tenders drawn above the waterline,
and catch her looking out to Tarner,
out to Wiay, further out to Uist.

Crows

What do the crows want with me?
They make such a racket
in the crazy Barnets of the winter trees.
Who said there was peace and quiet
in the countryside? There's never
a moment's peace here.
But the crows are the worst,
gossiping, arguing, fighting like fishwives.
They are even in my dreams.
Why do they land on me, walk
over my face and on my hands?
Why do they single me out?

Gifts of the Magi

Mary was all for burying the gold, saving it
for the rainy day she knew would come.
He said, why not live a little, it's not everyday
you celebrate the arrival of your first born?
Why not let your hair down for once?

They wrapped the frankincense in spare strips
of swaddling and some of the cleaner straw
and managed to take it all the way home
without incident. Him full of the spirit
and forgetting 'his troubles' is what did for it.

The myrrh was different, they agreed it should
be kept safe, though touch wood, they'd never
need it. For a time it sat on the mantelpiece
but it was put away when himself could reach it.
Mary never found out he sold it on the quiet.

The Census of Quirinius

I follow him down cold corridors,
our footsteps echoing around us,
him wringing his hands, the candles
flickering and the slaves mute and fearful.
He prefers the life of Rome to this dusty
backwater. I tell him: here is opportunity,
here you can make your mark and return
to the Sacred City a conqueror and hero.
He prevaricates, orders more rams
to be brought, hoping for a sign.
We have been given signs enough,
I want to say. The taxes are due,
the people owe their allegiance to Rome.
He is afraid to act, afraid of Joazar,
afraid to impose his will. He is weak.
He listens to the voices who whisper
from shadows, who sow doubts in him.
They tell him it's impossible to move
so many men, tell him I'll be forgotten,
a mere clerk. They underestimate me.
I'll be remembered for moving nations.

Robin's Last Arrow

The wounds at his wrists gape like the mouths
of men whose tongues he cut out
for swearing on the wrong oath. Marion sits
in the corner on a three-legged stool
watching the life drain out of him.

The arrow isn't his idea. She gives it to him, saying
let it fly like your soul into pits of hell
though your body will rest in the cool of the forest.
I was a good man once, he replies.
Pass me my bow and help me draw it.

Learning Magic

Look, look, the boy said, as he conjured flowers
from the air. The father smiled. Very nice.

And look, the boy said, making water
disappear inside a newspaper,

then making it pour into a jug.
Very impressive, the father said.

Now look, the boy said, levitating
and going too high. Be careful, the father said.

But look at this, the boy said,
juggling with knives. I don't like that

the father said. But look, this is even better,
the boy said, taking up three chainsaws.

You're frightening me, the father said.
But I can do this, the boy said, cutting off his arm

and then reattaching it, and the father said nothing;
he was too busy holding his breath.

A Portrait of the Artist
as a Sasquatch

Up in his lair
far from the hearts of men
he fingers the things
he's salvaged:
a left shoe, five unopened
labelless tin cans,
a broken radio.

It's not easy
hiding out in remote
locations,
being caught briefly
at the edge of shot
when camera shake
makes it hard to know
what's really there.

Later, while it's still light
he stands looking down
into the valley,
thinking of people
opening ready meals
and searching YouTube
for the latest sighting

before stretching out
to his full length of
eight to ten feet,
his eyelids drooping,
one enormous, hairy hand
twitching, while he dreams
of salt beef
and Shostakovich.

The Sore Thumb

When the water in the bay is flat, and clouds
        come off the Table
    like chimney smoke, we walk along the shore
and up through fields of grasses, and find ourselves
        near his place,
  so white it seems the stone is newly cut.
The breeze there drives the midges away
        and the outer isles,
    dark bergs from the shore, become the map's
archipelago. I've heard talk, at wakes and christenings,
        of a nod and a wink,
    that someone knew someone on the town planning
subcommittee. These days we see strangers here,
        German businessmen
    who want to try the island life, who smile and wave
at us. But mostly the windows are shuttered
        and the washing line
    is free to glint and clink against its posts.
Last week, though, we caught a rare glimpse
        on the path down
    to the beach. We spotted him in the distance,
his cagoule whipping in the wind, his bald head
        flashing like a gull's,
    and as we passed he paused, and turned
his hopeful face towards us, before someone said
        something appropriate,
    that we might slide by as by doe-eyed cattle
at the water's edge, that raise their heads,
        but never seem to low.

The Gift

Why? We don't know you, though we hear
     the rapid knocking of your voice through the wall,

and see you walking silently up the High Road
     ushering a gaggle of grandchildren before you,

maharani on an elephant swaying through the jungle.
     Sometimes you even raise an enigmatic smile,

then carry on, your turmeric yellow sari swinging
     under a three-quarter-length grey raincoat.

And then, one day, for no reason, a guttural eh eh eh
     and your hand over the trellis with a margarine tub

and a warm plastic bag. This first, then more,
     white grub-shaped things, sweetmeats, grey-green sauces

that taste hot-cold, sweet-sour, spicy-dry, so many
     flavours outside the language of our mouths. Now

to explain this: our reciprocation, banana bread,
     taken with a look of utter, utter bewilderment.

Noah to God

My grief moves like the sea, it carries me with it.
My nose is full of animal smells; I breathe the same hot air
the animals breathe. I feel their heat.

Salt works its way in everywhere. It scours our skin,
it makes our hair brittle, our hands crack.
Lions bed down with cattle, the elephant no longer moves.

I still hear the screams of my neighbours, my friends.
Their fear overwhelms me, and my heart
holds the sounds of their drowning children.

Maybe salvation is in the sad eyes of the zebra.

The Anaesthetist

It's a delicate business,
but trust me if you can.
Try to ignore my equipment -
it looks medieval I know,
all those tubes and masks,
the needle in your hand.

I could recite the names
of compounds and describe
to you their action in the blood,
could explain the calculations
based on body weight and age,
gender and medical history.

But what you suspect is true:
it is as much art as science,
this spinning out the thread
of life. How do you tell if it's drawn
too thin? you ask. It is a matter
of judgement, taste even.

So when you look me
in the eyes, and the cold
snakes its way up your arm
as you attempt to count to ten,
reassure yourself of this,
I will take care of you, I will -

My Son's Heritage

This is my son's heritage, not mine -
this church with its smoking candles

and the nun moving silently with her snuffer.
Where the women line up

with their hands crossed on their chests,
wearing long skirts, and their heads covered.

*

Old Metropolitan Anthony, ready to die,
who fought in the French Resistance,

held my face to the light when I met him,
This is Anna's granddaughter's fiancé.

He nodded, studied my face, and nodded.

*

I have no religion but I have a priest.
He walked with me across the park

from the Polish Club to the waiting cathedral.
I stood facing him on the end of the carpet

holding a candle, a cavern of light
behind me in the doorway. You forgot free will

said Deacon Peter by his side, you forgot
free will during the betrothal?

*

4am Easter morning.
We lay out the kulich and paskha

and shots of vodka, ready to break fast.

Bride and Groom Consume One Another

He couldn't help himself, he took a spoon
scooped out her right eye and swallowed it without chewing

she took a bite of his thumb, then finished off his whole left hand

he scattered fingernails over her hair and twisted the curls round his fork
before taking each breast whole into his mouth
having already snipped off her nipples with his two front teeth

she gnawed on his ears, making her way from one side of his skull to
                                       the other
then headed down, taking great chunks out of his arm

once he ran out of fingernails he snapped off her toenails
as quickly as he could, then buried his head between her legs
letting the juices run over what was left of his face

she took his penis in her mouth and swallowed it right down
to the root and she thought she might burst

but they kept going, each disappearing down the gullet of the other
until there was nothing left, no bones, no skin, not even a single eyelash.

Dance Mosquito

The night is hot, each hot room
        opening to another, and room to room
    we hunt a torturous mosquito,
                its whine drawing us from our bed
        where a baby, dough-armed, sleeps and sweats.
The sound vanishes into the wall's whiteness
    and we clamber after it
                over the green chaise longue
        and onto the Eucalyptus table
made from four railway sleepers.
        I watch you move, your violin curves.
                Your skin has a sheen to it
        like butter out of the fridge.
    The mosquito dances to his own tune
        lost in a different scale of forms and weights,
                the air's lifting current.
The night deepens, its hour unearthly.
        Our little victim can't hide too long.
                Before we dim the lights, you inspect
        the swat, the mangled legs, broken wings,
the long, infamous nose.

Carcasses

Fallen Angels

When God in his wrath
decided to punish the angels,
he turned them into gannets
and let them spend their lives
falling from the sky.

He made them perfect
from their stencilled beaks
to their rimless blue eyes,
from the gentle yellow dome
of their heads to their creaseless
                              feathers.

He set the sky on fire
and made the sea boil.
He used strips of solder
for fish and made the cliffs
a Chinese silkscreen print.

When we found one below
the line of bladder wrack
and rope and discarded plastic,
its neck cradled by rocks,
we were afraid to get too near.

Issigonis's Dream

In the dark, him and his boy
push the car to the edge
give it one more shove
then watch as it bounces
and lurches down the cliff
before finally settling
near the shore below
the MacDonald's place

the same MacDonald's
whose ancestors invited
the MacLeods to a church
at Trumpan for reconciliation
but instead shut them in
men, women, children, all
and razed the building
to the ground in vengeance.

Sunk in the swell
of bulrushes and reeds,
the Morris Minor
is a throwback to another age,
Issigonis's dream of luxury
for the working classes
in whose back seat
a generation of teenagers
pawed at each other
in the dying light.

Anatomy of a Whale

The whimsical light
               ignores the tide's
        foreboding, its shuck and hiss

                     the gulls' screams
the shrieking children.
             The coast's new moons

        gather minarets, sea arches
bone yards, the remnants
            of the battle-worn, battle-weary.

We are windburned
             hoarders after
        wrecked treasure.

               We search out
tusks of rib trapped
        between gabbro boulders

blunt stars of rumbled vertebrae
                  the bowed rostrum
            saw-toothed mandibles

and lug them all back
             Levites
        with the ark on our shoulders.

River in Spate

Yesterday we drove over the hill road where the sheep
ghost out of the mist, their black faces shockingly real,

to see the Snizort in spate. There is something shocking
about that too, in the churning of the peat-yellow water.

We were the only car to stop there and wonder at it.
The road simply goes between places, between the coasts

and even the few who choose to settle in the bog-land,
the soft belly of the island, don't choose to come here

where the road dips down to the river so if you time it right
you can make the kids' stomachs turn somersaults.

What I remember, though, is coming back in the early hours
and seeing a hind leap the deer fence, then disappear

into the forestry. But is that even possible - how much
of what we think we know is real? True or not,

I carry the image with me, her sinuous form caught
in the headlights, silvering like a salmon in its flight.

The Poet's Voice

The poet's voice quavers as she reads,
the paper in her hands trembling just a little.
She is wearing a long skirt that has fringing
and a blouse that has both lace and ruffles.
Her skin has the look of sponge cake dusted
with icing sugar. Her hair is maroon;
how the girl in the hairdressers described it
will forever remain a mystery.
The judge said that the images in the poem
were like a swarm of butterflies, touching down
so lightly they were gone before you grasped them.
They settle now on the heads in the room
and people blink like snow is falling.
She finishes and looks relieved; everyone claps.
It is a fine poem, and she is pleased with it.
She climbs down from the stage very carefully,
making sure each foot goes exactly where it should.

Skating at Earith

One winter in a score, it's cold enough
for the fens to freeze. Then they come from miles
around, the well-to-do, with fine-wrought skates,
the working men with blades from broken ploughs.
They compete for mutton and a sack of flour,
enough to feed a family for a month.
Year round the wind plays a single note
that maddens us with its sheer persistence;
there's nothing here to change its pitch, no hill
or craggy slopes, no rest from drawn-out lines.
Each man can see his father down the road.
Yet on the ice, no one is fixed in place;
two feet or less above the grass, all move
as if they've known a higher plane; here
is freedom of a kind. And when the race
has run and all return to winter tasks,
the working men to smiths and lathes, the squire
his lowland sports of snipe and hounds, that space,
that grand expanse of ice and sky is left
with ghosts of better, colder days. In summer,
when meadow grasses dance idly in the breeze
and trample-burrs catch at hems and stockings,
we try to picture skaters in these very fields
and hardly can believe it ever happened.

You're Letting Your Hair
Go Grey Again

You're letting your hair go grey again;
it's the autumn leaves that catch in trees.
You smoke cigarettes down to the ends.

There was once a reason to look the same
a friend, a lover to resist the change.
You're letting your hair go grey again.

People we know are sometimes friends
they sit with us on concrete steps.
You smoke cigarettes down to the ends.

You're not immune to the latest trends
though magazines are a daughter's habit.
You're letting your hair go grey again.

There's something in the way trees bend,
a lesson for those who want to see it.
You smoke cigarettes down to the ends.

The autumn colours are the deepest yet
they tell of summer's fires well spent.
You're letting your hair go grey again
and smoke cigarettes down to the ends.

The Bends

And let this be a lesson, frogmen,
to those who return too fast from a foreign element, the punishment
is terrible. Terrible for those like Icarus

who believe they've mastered the other place
with feathers glued to bamboo shoots, or prosthetic webbing.

Sojourners, be humble
as the earthworm is humble.

He embraces the earth, lets it pass through him, he burrows he eats
        his element,
blind, deaf, mute. He knows the vengeance of birds, their iron beaks.
So when you rise in a cacophony of bubbles

through the ocean's unmeasured mass,
come back slowly. Listen

to your breathing.
Think of the half-opened door of the moon, how it let slip
men into its bare pantry.

Of the tips of mountains and their time-lock on life,
and be thankful for yours.

A Gibbous Moon

Fat-bellied gibbous moon stares down at us
Lifts his head, blows raspberries at us
Thumbs his nose, shakes his arse at us
In and out of clouds, plays hide-and-seek with us
Puckers up and blows a kiss at us
Spreads his wares, out to make the most from us
Up-ends himself, wants to make a fool of us
Grows tired and tries to ignore the both of us
Swings long-armed star-to-star away from us
Glances back, takes one last look at us
Little fat-bellied gibbous moon, farewell from us

Acknowledgements are due to the editors of the following publications in which some of these poems, or versions of them, first appeared: *Acumen*; *The London Magazine*; *Magma*; *Orbis*; *Other Poetry*; *Outposts: Poetry News*; *Quattrocento*. 'The Sore Thumb' won the Poetry Society's Hamish Canham Prize in 2007; 'Eel' was highly commended in the Bridport Prize in 2015 and the Lumen and Camden Poetry Competition in 2016; 'Skating at Earith' was highly commended in the Ouse Washes Poetry Competition in 2016 and subsequently published in *The Fenland Reed*. 'Southampton in Paris' was commissioned for LiveCanon's Project 154 and published in the anthology of the same name in 2016. 'Hairy Panic' was long listed in the LiveCannon poetry competition in 2017 and published in the competition anthology. Some of these poems appeared in *Entering the Tapestry* (Enitharmon 2004) and in my pamphlet *The Bends* published by Eyewear in 2017.

Many thanks to Mathew Staunton & everyone at The Onslaught Press, and thanks to those who have given feedback on drafts of many of these poems, with special thanks to the Poetry School, and to Mimi Khalvati for her support and guidance over the years and feedback on the draft of this manuscript. Thanks also to the tutors and my fellow students on the Novel Studio for getting me writing again.

Other Onslaught Titles

Flower Press (2018) Alice Kinsella

Wings of Smoke (2017) Jim Pascual Agustin

Hold Your Breath (2017) Waqas Khwaja

Long Days of Rain (2017) Janak Sapkota

Orpheus in the Underpass (2017) Ross McKessock Gordon & Gabriel Rosenstock

ident (2016) Alan John Stubbs

the lightbulb has stigmata (2016) Helen Fletcher

Out of the Wilderness (2016) by Cathal Ó Searcaigh
with an introduction and translations by Gabriel Rosenstock

You Found a Beating Heart (2016) Nisha Bhakoo

I Wanna Make Jazz to You (2016) Moe Seager

Tea wi the Abbot (2016) Scots haiku by John McDonald
with transcreations in Irish by Gabriel Rosenstock

Judgement Day (2016) Gabriel Rosenstock

We Want Everything (2016) Moe Seager

to kingdom come (2016) edited by Rethabile Masilo

The Lost Box of Eyes (2016) Alan John Stubbs

Antlered Stag of Dawn (2015) Gabriel Rosenstock,
with translations by Mariko Sumikura & John McDonald

behind the yew hedge (2015) Mathew Staunton & Gabriel Rosenstock

Bumper Cars (2015) Athol Williams

Waslap (2015) Rethabile Masilo

Aistear Anama (2014) Tadhg Ó Caoinleáin

for the children of Gaza (2014) Mathew Staunton & Rethabile Masilo (eds.)

Lightning Source UK Ltd.
Milton Keynes UK
UKHW040629051219
354823UK00001B/87/P